Cotsw
Hillwalks

CHRISTOPHER KNOWLES

REARDON & SON
CHELTENHAM ENGLAND

Published by

REARDON & SON
Publishers
56 Upper Norwood Street, Leckhampton,
CHELTENHAM, GLOS. GL53 0DU

ISBN 0 9508674 5 4

Written and Researched by
CHRISTOPHER KNOWLES

Commissioned by
CHELTENHAM TOURIST INFORMATION CENTRE

Cover design, maps, illustrations by
Joanne Mathias
and
Peter T. Reardon

Printed by
LANCRESSE PRINTERS LTD
Staverton, Cheltenham, Gloucestershire.

INTRODUCTION

The following walks are designed to provide an introduction to the walking possibilities in the countryside around Cheltenham. All are circuitous so that a car can be parked at the point where the walk begins and ends. Where it is possible to reach the point of departure by bus, information is provided.

Some of the walks, inevitably, overlap a little, but repetition is only a fraction of any one walk. It is hoped that each of the walks has its own character and its own highlights, but that overall the walks contrive to give an insight into many of the charms of the Cheltenham area.

Efforts have been made to say something about what the walker is passing by and for those who prefer their walks to be accomplished at a leisurely pace, pubs are noted where they arise.

The going is not particularly hard, but there are a few reasonably steep slopes and plenty of lovely(!!) mud during wetter weather.

Finally, please remember to observe the basic rules of country walking:

Take nothing but photographs
Leave nothing but footprints
Kill nothing but time
And shut all gates behind you!

THE COTSWOLD WAY

This route was devised during the 1960's in order to give walkers almost one hundred miles of waymarked pathway and track across some of the most beautiful countryside in Britain. It is not an ancient route, but rather a concatenation of existing paths, some of which may be indeed of considerable antiquity. It stretches from Bath in the south to Chipping Camden in the north.

The comprehensive waymarking of the Cotswold Way, and indeed of many of routes in the area, is thanks to the dedication of the Rambler's Association and the Cotswold Voluntary Warden Service. The waymarks for the Cotswold Way are distinguishable from others by having a white dot placed by an arrow which is colour coded-yellow is a footpath, and blue a bridleway for walkers and riders. Some of the walks in this booklet overlap with sections of the Cotswold Way - its white dot will become a familiar landmark.

LECKHAMPTON HILL,
Nr CHELTENHAM. GLOS —

THE COTSWOLD QUARRIES

Much of the characteristic beauty of the Cotswolds comes from the limestone used in the construction of its local architecture. Unfortunately quarried limestone is usually too expensive to use these days, but the whole area is still pitted with disused quarries.

The limestone belt, of which the Cotswolds are a part, stretches from Dorset to South Yorkshire. Travelling the area reveals a wide variety in the colouring of the stone - this is dependent upon the amount of iron present in the rock.

One of the features of the area is its drystone walling. The method of creating a wall from loose stone dates back hundreds if not thousands of years, but the network that we see now, dates back to the 18th and 19th centuries after the introduction of the enclosure Acts.

Many of the older ones are crumbling away (consistent frost cracks them up) but rekindled interest in preservation is evident in the newly repaired walls. In the building of the walls, the stones, which are quarried from just a few feet down, are laid in courses and protected on top by a row of upright stones, known as combers.

Oolite freestone is found at a lower level in the quarry and is traditionally used for window surrounds and decorative sculpting, particularly in churches. Traditional roofing slates are made from limestone blocks which are easily split when exposed to frost this stone tends to be older still. They vary in size but are secured to the roof by means oak pegs through a hole in the top of the slate.

LECKHAMPTON HILL and the DEVIL'S CHIMNEY

Distance 3 miles

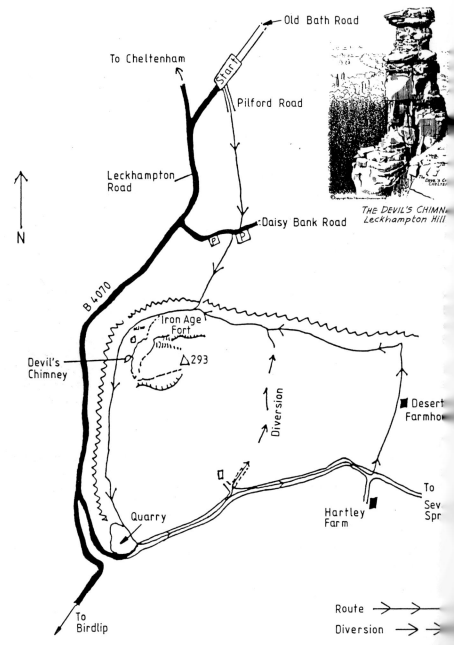

Old Bath Road

To Cheltenham

Start

Pilford Road

Leckhampton
Road

Daisy Bank Road

N

P P

B 4070

Iron Age
Fort

△293

Devil's
Chimney

Diversion

Desert
Farmho

Quarry

Hartley
Farm

To
Sev
Spr

To
Birdlip

THE DEVIL'S CHIMN
Leckhampton Hill

Route →→→
Diversion →→

Two Short Walks

Most of the walks in this guide require on average three hours to accomplish without undue exertion. In the case of some of the longer walks, short cuts will be indicated where feasible. Here are two circular walks that will take you no more that two hours.

Both walks are within striking distance of Cheltenham. In fact the first over Leckhampton Hill begins on the very edge of the town, whilst the second involves a short journey further east.

LECKHAMPTON HILL AND THE DEVILS' CHIMNEY

Ref: O.S. Landranger Series no. 163.
Start point - Grid Reference no. 949189

This walk of some three miles may be walked in 1-2 hours. Considering there are a couple of ascents and descents of moderate steepness, it is reasonably demanding but superb views and local lore are more than adequate compensation.

The basic route will take you around and over Leckhampton Hill, where you will be in touch with some of our earliest ancestors and bear witness to the triumph of good over evil.

The walk proper begins at Daisy Bank Road where there are car parking facilities.

If you are travelling by bus, take Metro Bus Route L. from the town centre to the stop at the junction of Old Bath Road and Leckhampton Road. They run approximately every 10 minutes starting at 7.00am and the last one returning to town at approximately 10.40pm. At time of print, there is no service available on Sundays or Bank Holidays. Bus times can however change, so please check with the Tourist Information Centre before your setting out on your walk.

Walking back along Old Bath Road for some 200 yards, you will reach Pilford Road on the right. At the far end of Pilford Road cross a stile and head up the field towards thorn bushes and on to a bank at the top of the meadow. Turn right along the bank to a stile on the left in the corner of the field. Cross this and another a few yards ahead into Daisy Bank Road and there, you will find the upper of the two car parking areas.

By Car: There are two car-parks on Daisy Bank Road. The first is larger and off the road on the right; the second is at the point where the walk begins and consists of a large lay-by, a few yards up the road from the first car park. If there is space, as there will be on week-days, use the first one (noting the BEWARE OF THE ADDERS sign!) and walk on to the second.

The Walk

At the second parking area, there is a stile on the right. Cross this and take the firm path upwards on a mild gradient towards the bulk of Leckhampton Hill. The path is wide and flanked by trees and banks that in season are sprinkled with flowers. Ahead is a sheer cliff of exposed Jurassic (185 to 135 million years ago) Oolitic Limestone (Oolites are the spherical grains which limestone is composed of.)

It was only sixty years ago that quarrying came to a halt at Leckhampton. Climbing to the level of the tree tops reveals excellent views of Cheltenham behind you. Soon the path levels out into a clearing, where signs of abandoned enterprise are much in evidence. A couple of crumbling stone kilns, a scattering of rock and boulder, and the gashes in the rock behind, are all that remain of the industry that during the 18th century provided the raw material, which when cut and polished, shaded and honed, became the building blocks of Regency Cheltenham.

CHELTENHAMS' ORIGINS

The derelict quarries of Leckhampton are notable in one other respect, for such was their importance all through the 19th century that they became the site of the first Cotswold railway which ran from the quarry to the city of Gloucester. At first the stone was hauled to kilns and down to the main road by means of a pulley system; later horse-drawn trams took their place and finally engine power did the job until the closure of the quarries in 1925. Many of today's paths originally carried railways of one sort or another, including the one that bought you up from the car park. That line ran from the quarry to Charlton Kings, now a suburb of Cheltenham. Rusted and bent rails still protrude uselessly from some of the boulders that litter the clearing.

Now continue up and around the hill keeping the cliffs on the left. Where the path opens out into a clearing, you will notice on your right two paths disappearing into the undergrowth. As it is somewhat steep, it is better to take the nearer of the two paths and proceed upwards in stages. After a fairly sharp incline, the path levels out on to a small ledge. Continue upwards passing a boulder on the left among the trees to another small ledge, with the cliff face (Dead Man's Quarry) clearly visible to the left.

The antiquity of the rock is revealed by different strata - from the bottom, the first 30 feet are pisolitic limestone, the next 75 of Lower Freestone, then 10 feet of Oolitic Marl, 30 of Upper Freestone and 25 of ragstone. Continue up to another larger ledge, with a bench well placed for looking at the fine views of Cheltenham. Follow the path as it winds between two hummocks onto another larger ledge with the plateau of Leckhampton Hill above you to your left. As you come through the cleft, look over the drop to the right for the irregular column of rock that is the 'Devil's Chimney'.

THE DEVIL'S COMEUPPANCE.

Its curious separateness cannot be attributed to nature and in the normal course of events it would have been quarried away. In about 1780 however, it was initially ignored by workmen because of the inferior stone quality and partly, perhaps, they colluded in the development of the legend that inevitably sprang up.

It seems that Gloucestershire was noted for having a surpassing number of churches and abbeys, much to the displeasure of the Devil. In his annoyance he hid on this ledge and extracting boulders from the rock with his trident, lobbed them towards the monks and pilgrims passing below. The power of good being greater than that of evil, the rocks, far from striking the hapless passers-by, came piling down instead on the Devil himself. Thus he schemes yet, but far beneath the quarry!

In the past it became custom for visitors to shin up to the top (the record apparently is 13 at one time.) but the practise, for the sake of climber and chimney, is now outlawed.

Between the Devil's Chimney and the next junction you have fine views of the Severn Valley. In the far distance is the Forest of Dean; the hill to the left is Robins Wood Hill (you can see the vertical line that is an artificial ski slope running down it) and Gloucester Cathedral is visible on a clear day.

Resuming the walk along the greensward, in about 100 yards you will meet junction of paths marked by a signpost pointing back to the Devil's Chimney. Ahead the path widens, with a field to its left and is ragged with gorse. The other path bears left up to the summit of Leckhampton Hill behind you. The walk takes you forward but if you wish to cover the site of the Iron Age fort then take the left path up and head back to the area above Dead Man's quarry, returning to the junction later.

THE INVISIBLE PAST.

There is little to see of the fort today - only the outer form with its commanding position. It would have covered the area from the edge of the plateau back to where the low ridge describes a shallow arc around it. Being single banked, the fort can be dated to the early Iron Age, about the 5th century B.C. Most of the many fortress remains of the Cotswolds date back to the Iron Age and although some are vast (up to 100 acres - this is a mere 7) they are to the contemporary eye nothing more than grassy banks. Excavation would disclose an altogether different aspect. There would be the remains of high drystone walls and before them, rock cut ditches. Behind these protective devices would have stood timber buildings, round and triangular, the nucleus of a village or camp. The smaller settlements like this one are thought to have been fortified residences of petty chieftains.

To resume the walk, return to the junction of the paths and the signpost to the Devil's Chimney, turning left onto the field with its sprinkling of gorse. Crossing this will bring you to a point where the path narrows and begins to descend towards a road. On your right you will pass another disused quarry below you. A short, sharp descent drops you on to a metalled road, a link road from the A435 to the B4070 road to Birdlip. Turn left here and keep to the metalled road for about half a mile. On your way you will pass signposts on the right to Coberley and Severn Springs, Ullenwood and Shurdington Hill which should be ignored. Beyond a cottage on your left, the road veers sharply to the right, whilst on the left is a track leading to farmyard buildings. Should you wish, the walk may be shortened at this point by taking this entrance and turning sharp right, where the track will take you towards a row of trees and the escarpment of Leckhampton Hill.

The walk proper continues along the metalled road where it veers right towards Hartley Farm which may be espied across the fields before you. The road is quiet and threads through rich, open farmland with recently repaired drystone walling to your right. The road divides the farm in two. On the right, just before the farm, a sign indicates a path, which you should ignore. Immediately after, still on the right, is the lane to the farm house and then an attractive old barn with a weather cock on its roof. On the left, pass a modern barn and then turn left just after into a yard. Ahead at about 150 yards, is the ruin of a building amidst a clump of trees, for which you should aim, crossing the stile before it, and leaving the track to meander away to the right. The building seems not to have been a byre, but, with its timbered fire-places still in place, it could have been a farm workers cottage.

Leave the ruin and continue a few yards on to another broken stile. You will probably find it easiest to turn left through the gate and then right to keep going forward, but in any case you should keep to the left of the fence heading for the row of trees ahead. Soon, as a stone wall appears on your left, you will find yourself in a defile which will eventually bring you out at another stile. Cross this and within a few strides you are on the long, coarse grass of Leckhampton Hill, amidst an abundance of bushes and stocky trees. Go forward a little for the main path and fine views across Cheltenham.

The walk proper goes left. Keep to the main path, which at a certain point, marked with a post with a blue arrow, bears left away from the escarpment edge, whilst another secondary path, to be disregarded, bears right and down under the brow of the hill. After 00 yards the path reaches a hummock marked with a waymarked post with a yellow arrow. Step up over this little rise and rather than following the main path ahead, turn immediately right, taking a narrower trail that heads towards a row of trees before bearing left and down steeply amidst woodland. After about 200 yards you will emerge just below the clearing with the old lime kilns, on to the track up which you first climbed at the beginning of the walk. Turn right and return to Daisy Bank Road.

PUB.

The nearest pub is the Wheatsheaf on the Old Bath Road, about 200 yards beyond Pilford Road.

UPLAND WALKWAY TO KILKENNY
O.S. Map - Landranger Series no.163
Starting point - Grid Reference no. 005185

This circular walk is roughly the same length as the previous one, some three and a half miles, and should take no longer than two hours. The character is wholly different. Whereas on Leckhampton Hill you were often on a windswept common, here you are still high on the Cotswold escarpment (up to 1000 ft) but the views are hinted at, rather than lavishly presented, the atmosphere is of solitude but not loneliness, and the contrasts are subtle rather than marked.

There is no escaping the mud at certain times, but since you are mostly on high ground, the routes are comparatively dry and the only time that you are in a dell, where the damp might make the going sticky, the path is a metalled road.

The Start.

If you are travelling by Bus: 'Pulhams' run a service from Cheltenham to Bourton-on-the-Water and Moreton-in-Marsh, starting at approx. 9.30am. Alight at Andoversford and walk 1 mile to Kilkenny along the A436.

By Car: Park in the car-park/picnic area just off the A436 (signposted Kilkenny Viewpoint) near the radio masts just west of the Kilkenny pub.

The Walk.

Leave the car park the same way by which you entered (under the height trap) and turn left on to Hilcot road, the minor road linking the car park to the main road. At this point you are surrounded as far as the eye can see, by agricultural Gloucestershire. As you walk up towards the radio masts on your left, there will be glimpses of Cheltenham to your right. A little further right is Cleeve Hill, the highest point of the Cotswolds (recognisable by a set of three radio masts amongst the pylons). To your left there are views across the valley to acres of land under cultivation, that climb up to a long ridge spiked with tight knots of woodland at irregular intervals. Behind you are the villages of Dowdeswell and Upper Dowdeswell. After about 100 yards you will notice a spinney of larch trees in a field to the left - this is St Paul's Epistle, so called after the custom of reading biblical passages whilst beating the bounds of Dowdeswell parish. St Paul in particular finds favour at this high spot because of his cry for faith to spread over all the world. For most people until the recent past, the world consisted only of the horizon seen from the nearest high place.

You will be following a wooden rail to the left - where this ends in a series of posts and an odd looking triangular jump, immediately before a strip of beech woodland, turn left over a stile into a field. This is a bridle path junction, indicated with signs. Once in the field bear right around the corner of a walled thicket, and over a stile towards a small fenced mound, a covered resevoir. To the left you look across the Coln Valley. The Coln, which is crossed by the Fosse Way further south, passes through such picturesque villages as Bibury and joins the Thames at Fairford.

UPLAND WALKWAY
Distance 3½ miles

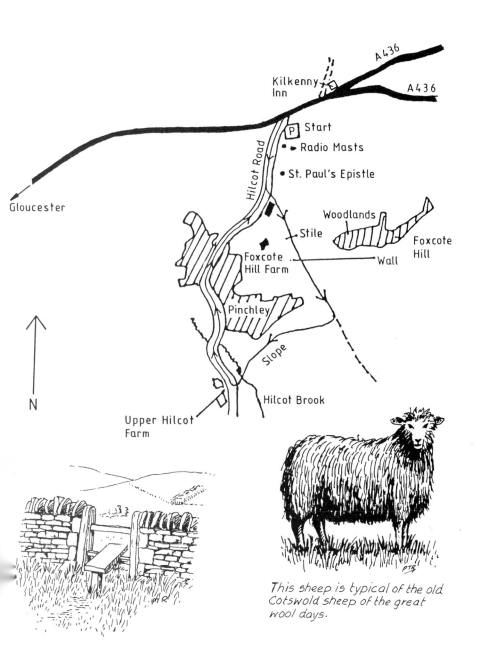

A436

Kilkenny Inn

A436

P Start

Radio Masts

St. Paul's Epistle

Hilcot Road

Gloucester

Woodlands

Stile

Foxcote Hill

Foxcote Hill Farm

Wall

Pinchley

Slope

N

Hilcot Brook

Upper Hilcot Farm

This sheep is typical of the old Cotswold sheep of the great wool days.

NOTHING IS AS IT SEEMS.

To look about you at the fields, farmhouses and woodland, is to feel that all is as it should be, that the shape of the land as defined by boundaries and natural features, is more or less immutable. Yet, this is a false impression and over the centuries, there have been certain changes in the uses to which the land has been put. Two hundred years ago, much of the land would not have been under cultivation at all, but given over to sheep pasture. It is all a question of economics. Originally, much of the area of the Cotswolds would have been covered with decidious woodland. With the arrival of the first farmers, clearings were made and the first crops planted. Populations grew and larger areas of woodland were uprooted, until by the 14th century, the open field system of arable farming was pre-eminent. At the same time the wool trade was in the ascendant, so that large areas became sheep pasture. With the Enclosure Acts of the 18th and 19th centuries, at least 120,000 acres of land were enclosed with hedge or drystone walling, since when the landscape has changed little.

Keeping the wall to your right, continue walking forward. You will see another wall running across the land in front of you, and where the two meet there is a stile. Beyond, a field rises up to a hedge, some 350 yards distant, and has a row of pylons running its length. Cross this stile and press on ahead (you may find yourself in a part of the field that has been fenced off as a sheep fold) between pylons and the stone wall. Another wall lies in front and as you approach it, look left to a pleasing strip of green that dives, with all the pace of a race course, between the wall and a piece of woodland. Once again, pass through the wall and carry on, still keeping the other wall on the right. This wall becomes wooden railings, at the end of which is a string of conifer trees. At this point the rail reverts to stone wall and hinges left for a wooden bridle gate. Pass through, turn sharp right, right again through another gate and immediately left, walking straight along the left margin of the field with woodland and the conifers to your left. Follow the tracks as it dips and rises. After the woodland has completely thinned out to the left, there are views of a farmhouse beyond a row of cypresses - its garden has a charming array of ornamental trees. Also to the left, but further across the valley to the right, in a hollow, is a beautiful timbered farmhouse - this is Upper Hilcot Farm. After some 250 yards, you come to another gate, distinguished by a black arrow on a white background with green surround. Go through this gate and away with the path as it bears down and slightly left under the sizzling pylons. This area is known as ''Smoke Acre'', a name derived from land originally held by payment of money, known as 'smoke pennies', in place of tithewood.

Soon you will meet another stile, again carrying the black arrow, in the left corner by some trees. Once over the stile and as the scrub thins out, there are pretty views along a narrow valley to the left. After another 100 yards, there is another stile leading away to the left. Cross and follow a thin grassy track as it plunges down the bank into the valley below. At a certain point the track bears right (there should be a yellow waymark) - follow this until you come to a gate, also waymarked, that leads into part of a farmyard. Ahead is Upper Hilcot Farm and to the right an attractive pool, part of Hilcot Brook. Continue along the track until you meet a gate and then a metalled road. This is Hilcot Lane. Turn right keeping the farmhouse and converted barn on your left, and walk down to where a little stone bridge arches over Hilcot Brook. Follow the road which leads eventually back to the car-park. Some 250 yards ahead, the road enters woodland (note the sign pinned to one of the trees 'Private Woods'). These are Pinchley Woods, the word Pinchley meaning 'the clearing frequented by finches'. At one point the bank to the left falls away steeply - its name, 'Breackneck Bank', needs no further explanation.

Half a mile ahead the woodlands give way to open fields. Where the road rises and straightens out, a lane on the right leads to imposing Foxcote Hill Farm. Opposite, a sign indicates 'Keeper's Cottage'.

Carry straight on until you meet the point where you turned off the road near the beginning of the walk. Continue past this and the radio masts, until the car park comes into sight.

PUB.

The nearest pub is the Kilkenny. Turn right out of Hilcot Lane on to the main road and it is about a quarter of a mile down the way on the left. Good food is served at the appropriate times.

A FORD AT SHIPTON OLIFFE IN GLOUCESTERSHIRE.

CLEEVE COMMON and POSTLIP HALL
Distance 5 miles

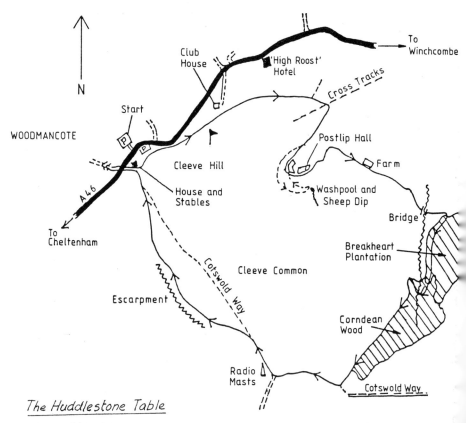

N

WOODMANCOTE

Start

Club House

'High Roost' Hotel

Cross Tracks

To Winchcombe

Cleeve Hill

House and Stables

A46

To Cheltenham

Postlip Hall

Farm

Washpool and Sheep Dip

Bridge

Breakheart Plantation

Cleeve Common

Cotswold Way

Escarpment

Corndean Wood

Radio Masts

Cotswold Way

The Huddlestone Table

The legend has it that after the dedication of the Abbey of St Peter at Winchcombe, Kenulf, King of the Mercians bade farewell to King Cuthred and various dignitaries at this spot, and the Huddlestone Table was set up, apparently, on the site of an earlier similar monument

O.S. ref SO 984253

Cleeve Common: Two Walks

The following two walks have Cleeve Common as their starting points. They overlap slightly but, in the main, each covers different parts of the common and different routes. Both are longer than the preceding two and will require more time and energy. Both, however, offer tremendous contrasts, fine views, houses or castles, and seclusion.

The first and shorter of the two is a more rugged walk, whilst the second is somewhat longer, but more gentle in character, and could make an excellent day's outing.

THE HILL AND THE COMMON.

Since the walks begin at the Common itself, some general information about it covers them both.

Cleeve Hill forms part of the westerly escarpment of the Cotswolds. At 1083 ft, it is not only the highest point of the Cotswolds, but the highest in lowland England. Almost wherever you go in the Cheltenham area, it is possible to catch a glimpse of it, recognisable even at a distance by the three radio masts that stand like sentinels on its edge.

The common covers a large are of the plateau part of the escarpment. It is some 3 square mils in area, roughly 1250 acres and is the last tract of the wild grazing land, similar to what would have covered much of the area before the Enclosure Acts in the 18th and 19th centuries. It still serves as common grazing land; but since the common is listed as a Grade 1 site of special scientific interest, the limestone grassland has every chance of throwing up more exquisite delights, like musk, frog and bee orchids, glow worms, striped winged grasshoppers, butterflies, skylarks as well as the ubiquitous gorse bush, and the broom and tor varieties of grass.

The common is not exclusively of interest to scientists and naturalists, nor is it frequented simply by walkers. Par of the area is devoted to a public gold course and the gallops, still in use, were the same along which great jockeys like Fred Archer and Tom Oilver thundered on their thoroughbreds. It is therefore a place of many and potential conflicting interests. It is a delicate balance, but such conflicts are lost in the vastness of the common and in its wild seclusion.

CLEEVE COMMON and POSTLIP HALL - THE FIRST WALK.

O.S. Landranger Series no. 163
Starting Point Grid Reference no. 982268

In which you leave behind the fairways and plunge down to the picturesque Postlip Hall; tread carefully through Breakheart Plantation; remount Cleeve Common and traverse its windy plateau. A circular walk of some 5 miles which will require approximately 3 hours to complete. There are a couple of short steep climbs and mud is likely to be plentiful in the winter.

Arriving by Bus: Castleways of Winchcombe operate a frequent service from Cheltenham to Winchcombe. Alight at Rising Sun Hotel on Cleeve Hill and walk up to the car-parks some 400 yards ahead.

By Car: There are a couple of parking areas on the A46 see map. Walk back down the hill past some toilets on the left, until you come to a stile by a gate with a yellow arrow.

Once over the stile, head directly up the side of the slope. Bear left round a house and stables, so that you are walking above them, with an iron railing on your left. On your right is a golf fairway, part of Cleeve Hill Municipal Golf Course. Continuing ahead, extensive views of Woodmancote, Bishops Cleeve, (whose Norman church is one of the largest and most splendid in the country, with a beautiful Jacobean musician's gallery) and the Vale of Gloucester are evident on your left. Soon a disused quarry will appear below you to your left. Looking out across the vale, in the far distance, the Tower of Tewkesbury Abbey should be visible. A little further along, you will come to the proverbial 19th hole, or the golf clubhouse, which has a bar open to the general public. Snacks are available too and in the winter months, a roaring fire warms your feet under the wooden tablets on the wall that catalogue recent presidents and captains.

As for the walk, continue past the clubhouse, ignoring the road that leads away to the left, walking straight on with a wall to your left and a fairway to the right. In front, wooded hillsides and the sizeable town of Winchcombe come into view, nestling between two hills slightly to the left. After some 300 yards there will be, or what was, a fenced-in vegetable patch to the left and a gate ahead of you, which you should pass through on to a firm track that pierces rows of stubby bushes and trees. Ignore the gate with the yellow arrow that will appear on the left. At the end of this track, you will come to a gate that brings you to a crossroads, where you should head forward but slightly right and diagonally down the slope. Head for a gate amongst some trees in a shallow corner at the bottom, ignoring a path that runs across the oblique of the slope to the left and right.

DIVERSION.

At this juncture of the walk, you may wish to take a small diversion (a further 20/30 minutes walking). Instead of going through the gate, turn right before it and continue by a wall running alongside a sparsely wooded meadow (part of the Postlip Estate) to your left. Follow the wall for some 250 yards until it curves around to the left. As the curve begins to straighten up, you will see a stile leading into the woods on your left, which, for the time being, is to be ignored. Carry straight on along the main path, disregarding a track to the left. After 100 yards, you will come to a pool, backed by some wild slopes - this is the Washpool, fed by a stream, which has its course further up the valley. The unusual keyhole shaped pit below the pool is an old sheep dip. Several varieties of orchid are supposed to grow in this part of the common.

To rejoin the walk, retrace your steps to the stile, leading into the woods. Cross this and follow the path through the trees, with a stream to the right. After a few yards, you will see a post waymarked with a yellow arrow, which will bring you into a meadow. Walk across the middle of the field towards a gate marked with another yellow arrow. Go through this first gate and then after 30 yards, another that will bring you back on to a track along side a high stone wall surrounding Postlip Hall. Turn right here. You have now rejoined the main walk (see Postlip Hall below and then following paragraph).

If you have decided against taking the diversion, go through the gate described as being in a shallow corner amidst the trees. It has 'Private: footpath only' written on but is open to walkers. you will find yourself on a track with a high stone wall on the left and pasture, with a sprinkling of trees, to the right. Behind the wall is a charming gathering of old English architecture that comes, perhaps as something of a surprise, after the comparative wilderness of Cleeve Common. This is Postlip Hall.

POSTLIP HALL.

Almost invisible, hemmed in as it is on three sides by hills, Postlip Hall nevertheless is of a commanding aspect. It is thought that the name Postlip is derived either from 'Pott's chasm' or a 'declivity near a deep hollow'. There are three principal buildings grouped together. The first that is visible to you is the Roman Catholic chapel, dedicated to St. James, thought to be the oldest in the county. Parts of it date back to the 12th century. The Reformation brought its desecration - it is said to be scarred with bullet marks from the Civil War. For many years this stubborn little bulwark of Roman Catholicism became a barn until it was reconsecrated in 1891. Beyond it, is the Hall, built on the site of a man belonging to one Robert de Solers, dating back to the 16th and early 17th centuries. The third building, more easily seen as you make your way around the grounds, is a marvellous tithe (the word tithe comes from the Old English meaning 'tenth' and refers to a tax usually payable in kind) barn dating back to the 15th century. Later, as you pass the entrance to the Hall, you can see an effigy atop the barn, said to be in the likeness of Sir William of Postlip, son of Robert de Solers. The Hall is now a commune and events, such as beer festivals take place here from time to time.

Continue along the path, snatching glimpses of the chapel and hall where you can. On the left, notice the old wooden gate posts and on the right, the ancient well spring in the meadow. Follow the wall round to the left (at this point walkers who opted for the diversion should rejoin the trail), and pass through two gates on to a track that on the right leads to the stables and a converted mill, complete with wheel, and to the left through the wall to the hall. You are not allowed to enter the grounds here, but a fine view of the barn is on offer. Cross the track, go through a small wooden gate and entering a field, follow the wall round to the left. By climbing a little way up the hill to the right, you can obtain good views of the hall; otherwise peer through gaps in the wall and strike on until you come to a gate leading on to a metalled road. Ahead a path leads down to Postlip Mills and on to Winchcombe. To the left is an entrance to the Hall and to the right the route you are to follow. Below you in the valley, steam may be seen to rise from the paper mill on the River Isbourne - and the rising road will take you past a house and into a farmyard.

Go through the farmyard towards a gateway, ignoring another on the right. passing through the first gate will reveal a firm track running alongside a wire fence on the left and turn immediately right towards the woods at the bottom, so that the fence is now to your right. Follow the field down looking to the left towards the village of Winchcombe. At the bottom cross the gate to a stream and the ancient stone slabs that ford it. Cross the stream and take the path that bears right up into the trees, keeping the stream to the right. This is quite a sharp ascent, but as it winds round to the left, recent clearing of trees allow broad views behind you. As the path rises and leaves the stream behind, head for a gate that appears before you slightly to the left and enter a field. Keep left and head for a stile in the left hand corner. Crossing it will leave you on a small road, from where there are good views to Winchcombe and towards the Vale of Evesham, as well as of Postlip Hall.

The illustrious building below you, to the right of Winchcombe, is Sudeley Castle (for information about both Winchcombe and Sudeley Castle, see the second of the Cleeve Common walks.)

Turn right along this road, obeying the sign to Cleeve Common, passing a low building on the right, and ignoring a path into the undergrowth on the left. Soon the road peters out into a sort of fork. On the right it becomes the drive of a house called 'Woodpeckers'. On the left it becomes a track that takes you into Breakheart Plantation. Take this track as it dips and then rises gently through the plantation, the stream reappearing to your right, buttressed by remains of an old wall and above it, the slopes of Cleeve Common. Felling and clearing of trees is likely to be taking place on occasions, which may result in the muddying of the path and the presence of unexpected clearings. In such cases a little scouting will locate the direction of the true path. Eventually you will arrive in a small clearing and a meeting of paths. A post with yellow arrows indicates several possibilities - but you should bear right for 50 yards until meeting another junction. Ignore the arrow there pointing you to the left, and instead turn right. Entering the woods again, you will come across, after some 50 yards, a spring emanating from the bank on the left, and a hut to the right with a cistern to its rear containing water of a miraculous limpidity, considering the piping rusting in its depths.

About 15 yards beyond the hut, just before a mossy and dilapidated stone wall, there is a narrow and fairly steep path that goes left up the wooded hill. Follow it up until you are once again on the long grass of Cleeve Common, albeit on the slopes below the plateau. Emerging from the woods, bear left along an indistinct path at about the level of the tree tops to your left. On a sunny day, even in winter, the grass reflects gold, like straw, and the trees are purple and deep green.

Continue on, ignoring a path leading up to a gate on your right and following the path which runs around the base of the slope close to the edge of the woods and then straightens out to run across the oblique of it. Gradually the woods and the hill whose slope you are traversing part company, exposing a strip of green at the base of the hill. Eventually the path will force you down there, and just after, at the point where you see a gate leading back into the woods on the left, you will see a grassy track, a cleft between folds of the hillside, leading up to the summit of the common on the right. Take this until a trio of radio masts appear to your left. Thread your way through the gorse bushes towards them and then turn right hugging the fence to the left. Here, at or close to the highest point of the Cotswolds, you are on a windswept plain inhabited by lone horsemen and distant walkers, surrounded by some of the most fabulous views in the county.

Having turned right at the masts, continue on. By following the edge of the escarpment, you will eventually return to the house and stables where the walk began. Follow the stone wall on the left. Soon the famous racecourse at Prestbury will appear below you. Advance along the edge of the common, ignoring any stiles and gates to the left. Eventually you will notice what appears to be cliffs, that are the result of quarrying below you. This is Cleeve Cloud (from the old English 'edge of the rock outcrop'), which was an Iron Age fort much of which has, indeed, been quarried away. Castle Rock, popular with rock climbers, is at the end of this outcrop and is the largest area of exposed rock in the Cotswolds. Before you to the west are the Malvern Hills and the Black Mountains.

Continue forward until the golf fairways begin to veer away to the right and the escarpment edge descends in front of you. There are houses below you on the left and a bewildering array of paths and tracks run haphazardly across the Common and its broken slopes. However, you will notice that one track, rather wide and sunken, appears to maintain a steady course forward. Following this will take you in the right direction, until a point where is bears left. Continue forward here, until some houses appear before you, and the stables near where you started the walk are clearly visible on the right. To its left is a stile that will take you to the main road.

PUB.

The nearest pub within walking distance is the High Roost (Free House), which offers fine views across Cheltenham. Food is served here. Turn right along the main road after the stile and walk for about a quarter of a mile.

CLEEVE, SUDELEY and WINCHCOMBE - THE SECOND WALK.

O.S. Landranger Series no. 163
Starting Point Grid Reference no. 982268

In which you will explore the wilder reaches of Cleeve Common; creep through a deserted farm; wonder at a mass grave; marvel at a fabled castle; pass an ancient town; see the last vestiges of an industry imported from China and glimpse an historical manor.

This is the longest walk in the guide, a circular one of about 8 miles, which would take about 4 - 5 hours at an even pace. However, it is also the least rugged and combined with visits to Sudeley Castle (when open), or the town of Winchcombe, would be a fine way to spend a day immersed in various aspects of the Cotswolds.

Arriving by Bus: Castleways of Winchcombe operate a frequent service from Cheltenham to Winchcombe and back. Alight at the Rising Sun Hotel on Cleeve Hill.

By Car: Park in one of the two places provided (see map) and walk back down the road, ignoring the gate leading to a house and passing the public toilets on your left. You will quickly come to a gate and stile.

Go on to the common here, head straight up the slope and bear left around a house and stables so that you are walking above them with an iron railing on your left side. On the right is a golf fairway, part of Cleeve Hill Municipal Golf Course. As you continue, you will have good views of the villages of Woodmancote and Bishop's Cleeve to the left. Soon a disused quarry will appear below you to the left and splendid views will extend across the vale of Tewkesbury and its Abbey.

Walk on to the clubhouse (open to the public for drinks and snacks). Just past it, notice a wide track leading away to your right, at a slight angle behind you, across the fairway. This track cannot be confused with any other since at its beginning there are traffic signs that forbid entry to cars and motor-cycles. Ignore the track that forks away to the right. You will be keeping to this path for some time, passing a maintenance hut on the right. You will be able to see that cluster of radio masts lying ahead. Although it will be unnecessary to go right up to them, they provide a convenient marker and you go for the time being in their general direction. The track bears to the right and down through an area of gorse and then left across a wide hollow where you should watch out for golfers teeing off to your left and right. Once you leave the fairways behind, the path becomes less obvious, but if in doubt head for the radio masts. This part of the common is beautiful in its windswept solitude, with the gorse providing a low forest of prickly perches for the birds.

As the path continues onwards, the gorse spreads out to the left and the common opens out to the right; and as the masts get nearer, so the path becomes a pale strip of grass. Follow this over the brow of a low hill, ignoring all other paths that may appear to the left and right. Once over the brow continue until you are level with the masts and head for a patch of gorse ahead of you. The path cleaves through the gorse and takes you down towards a broken down stone wall, behind which a line of pylons is strung out along an area of farmland. Head for a gate and the remains of a cattle grid in the stone wall. Go through the gate into a field and follow the track up and them down to a deserted farm. You are now on arable land which makes a striking contrast with the desolate common behind. At the bottom of the field, the path will take you through a gate and then down to old Wontley Farm. This is a traditional assembly of Cotswold farm buildings, redundant but intact, dating back to the 18th century, when much of the land in the area was devoted to sheep farming. There are three buildings altogether - the first on the left, with two floors, appears to have been a sheep-shearing shed below and perhaps a wool store, and granary, above. In front of you are the old stables. The largest building would seem to have been a storage

19

CLEEVE, SUDELEY and WINCHCOMBE
Distance 8 miles

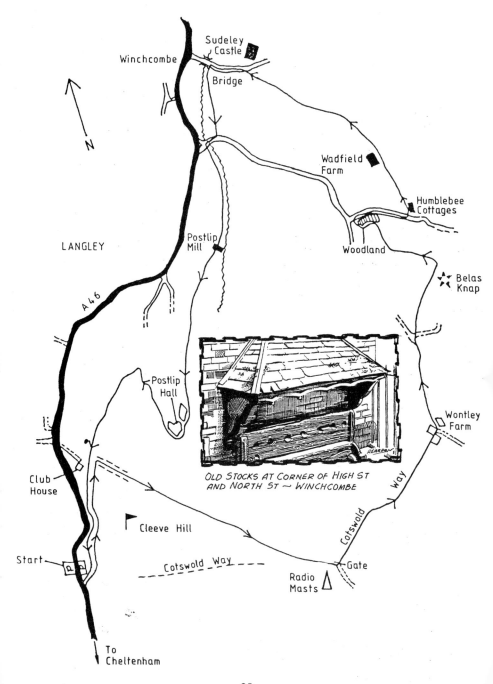

Winchcombe

Sudeley Castle

Bridge

Wadfield Farm

Humblebee Cottages

N

LANGLEY

A46

Postlip Mill

Woodland

Belas Knap

Postlip Hall

Wontley Farm

Club House

Cotswold Way

Cleeve Hill

Cotswold Way

Gate

Radio Masts

Start

To Cheltenham

OLD STOCKS AT CORNER OF HIGH ST AND NORTH ST ~ WINCHCOMBE

barn - the interior is rather impressive, and the walls have a good deal of graffiti carved into them, some of which claims to date back to the 18th century!

Continuing the walk, turn left after the first building and follow the path through a gateway (it has a white arrow on it) with a cattle grid to one side, on to a good firm track that has a wall to its left and an open field to the right. Keep going for half a mile until the path is lined on either side with small trees immediately before a junction, where a signpost indicates Belas Knap and Winchcombe to the right (although this signpost sometimes points, incorrectly, ahead of you). The correct path runs along a field on the other side of a broken wall to your right and in case there is any doubt, a stone gatepost on the path ahead of you has an arrow pointing you in the direction you want. Once on this path, with an open field to the right and hedges to the left, a low grassy mound, a little too symmetrical to be natural, will appear some way in front of you. The path comes to an end at a stile over which you enter the enclosure of Belas Knap ('beacon hill') long barrow, which dates back to 2000 B.C. and is the finest example of a New Stone Age false-entrance barrow in the Cotswolds.

BELAS KNAP.

Certainly these barrows were used for burial purposes, but they cannot be considered as cemeteries since the number of skeletons found is generally disproportionate to the size of the mound (in this case 38 bodies in a construction that was originally some 200 by 80ft). Nor were they the final resting places of princes and kings, judging by the way in which the corpses were unceremoniously thrown together. Rather, it is thought that they were sacred places where gods of life and death were ritually placated, and that therefore the skeletons found here are the remains of chieftains and priests.

Their construction was a remarkable feat of early engineering by what was essentially a society of subsistence farmers. It is thought that 15,000 man-hours may have been needed to build what is a huge cairn of stones complete with internal passages, chambers and drystone-faced walls. Barrow building, it is considered, fell into three categories during the Neolithic era - this, the 'false-portal' type with side chambers, may have come about as a deterrent to grave robbers. Details about the construction and layout of the barrow are given on a plaque opposite the main portal.

From the stile you last crossed, continue on, with the barrow to the right, to another stile in the left corner. Cross this and turn immediately left through a swing gate, after which you bear left again, along a path into a field, where you turn right, following a thicket that hides a crumbling wall. This chunk of woodland has the charming name of 'Humblebee How' (corrupted from an earlier word meaning 'scarred scree hillside') and is mostly composed of hawthorn, larch and pole ash.

The field dips down ahead and views of Cleeve Common open up to the left. Follow the curve of the field, ignoring a little locked gate on the right. Keep the wall to the right, and in a corner, as you approach another field, is a swing gate. Go through and follow the path down, keeping the wall to the right. Follow the perimeter of the field as it bears to the left alongside a wood. At this point where a small tree-lined gully comes in from the left, you will see a swing gate on the right that leads into the wood. The path takes you steeply and quickly down to a stile and a metalled road, Cordean Lane, where you turn right. Shortly after taking this road, the woods give way to open fields, with more woodlands ahead. Before entering this little forest (Humblebee How, yet again), you will see a sign on the left for the Cotswold Way and Humblebee Cottages, which offer Bed & Breakfast. Take this path down past the cottages. To the left of the track are the remains of a Roman Villa discovered during ploughing in 1863. For access to this you need to ask at Humblebee Cottage.

Follow the track as it bears left towards Wadfield Farm ('Wadfield' comes from the 'woad field', woad being a plant that produced a blue dye used in the woollen industry). Do not enter the farmyard, but continue past the house, walking towards two green gates in the fence before you. Take the stile with the yellow arrow and head towards the distant castle, following a normally well trimmed hedge on the right. Continue down to another waymarked stile, placed between the hedge and a tree. Cross this and follow the field around to the left (ignoring a gate in the corner) until you come to another stile on your right, just after the point where a row of trees thins out. Cross this into a field and turn left. Very quickly the path turns to the right and then within a few yards you will see on the left a brook, a little bridge and a stile. Cross into the field which has a broad track running right diagonally through the crops. If the track is unclear, aim for the leftermost of the telegraph poles or in the rough direction of the church. At the end of the track you will reach another stream, bridge and stile and beyond them, another field where the track that you want, runs across diagonally right. The church remains a convenient marker if the path is hard to locate.

Close to the far corner of this field is yet another stream, bridge and stile. Crossing them will bring you into a grassy field rising ahead of you. You head for the telegraph pole with a white sign affixed. As you reach the brow of the field, Winchcombe church is clearly visible ahead of you and there is a stile leading on to a road in the far right hand corner. Once on the road, turn left towards Winchcombe. It curves right and left towards Winchcombe. It curves right and left past the Almsbury Lodge entrance of Sudeley Castle, built in 1893.

SUDELEY CASTLE.

Sudeley Castle dates back to 1398, but is not a craggy fortress of the middle ages, but rather an elegant country house adorned with stylised turrets and crenellations.

Sudeley ('clearing with a shed') was mentioned in the Domesday Book, but the first castle on the current site, or in close proximity, was not built until the 12th century. Two centuries later, a member of the Boteler family (William Lord Boteler of Wemme) married Joan de Sudeley, thus acquiring the estate. By 1450, the first substantial castle on this site had been built. No sooner had the Boteler family stood back to admire their handiwork than the War of the Roses flared up.

The head of the family backed the wrong horse which led to the property being granted to the Duke of Gloucester by Edward IV. During the reign of Henry VIII, Sudeley became a royal seat. He was certainly an occasional visitor but it is with the last of his six wives, Katherine Parr, that the Castle is particularly connected. Following the King's death, she married Sir Thomas Seymour who had been granted ownership of Sudeley in 1547. The following year she gave birth to a daughter here and died a few days later. She is buried in the adjacent St. Mary's Chapel.

Subsequently, the estate came into the hands of the first Lord Chandos whose alterations in Tudor style largely produced the aspect that the castle wears today. One of his descendants backed the wrong horse again in the Civil War, after which the castle, with its desecrated chapel, lay rotting until its purchase by the Dent family (who had become prosperous through the manufacture of gloves) in 1863. It was completely restored through their good offices, to the extent that period dramas are occasionally filmed in the grounds.

Please check for exact opening times and details of events.

After the entrance to the Castle, the road passes a charming old farmyard (still in use): ahead are attractive houses, a bridge across the River Isbourne, and Winchcombe church. The walk turns left through a swing gate just before the bridge, but a convenient stop could be made at this delightful Cotswold village. The nearest pub is the Plasterer's Arms which is found by following the road ahead of you to the junction with the high street and turning right.

WINCHCOMBE

The meaning of the name of this town is 'valley with a bend in it' from the Old English. It is thought that King Offa (of Offa's Dyke fame) lived here. Certainly he founded a nunnery here in about 790 AD, and not long after, a King Kenulf founded an abbey upon which the town's subsequent prosperity was based. It was Kenulf's son, Kenelm, who was adopted as a saint and to whom generations of pilgrims came to pay their respects.

The fortunes of the abbey rose and fell, but towards the beginning of the first millennium AD, the founding of Benedictine orders in the area saw its importance attain new heights. Not many years after, Winchcombe, growing in importance alongside the abbey, was at one stage the capital of the short lived Winchcombeshire, which after twenty years became part of the greater shire administered from Gloucester. Winchcombe Abbey continued to prosper, however, until 1539 and the dissolution of the Monasteries under Henry VIII. Its former location is marked by Abbey Terrace in the heart of the old town.

With the fall of the abbey, for so long the conduit of the town's prosperity, the inhabitants were at a loss. Dependence on income generated by the abbey had bred a certain complacency in the town so that, unlike many of its near neighbours, it had never become a great centre for the wool industry. Ventures came and went - tobacco was successfully grown throughout much of the 17th century, but could not compete with the recently settled colony of Virginia. Gradually Winchcombe fell into a quiet repose, relying on the prowess of local farmers.

Back to the walk .... turn left through the swing gate into a field with the river Isbourne on the right. The Isbourne rises on Cleeve Common and. one of the few rivers in the county to flow northwards, joins the Avon at Evesham. Follow the faint path until you come to a gate and stile. Taking the stile brings you into a defile between a hedge and a fence, which you carry through until you meet a road (Corndean Lane). Turning right, go down the lane to where a small bridge spans the River Isbourne. The lane meets a loop road from the A46. A road sign tells you that Cleeve Hill is 2 miles away; and a path sign by a gate to the left indicates that Cleeve Common lies one and three quarter miles distant. Thus turn left at the bridge end and, crossing the stile, follow the path to Cleeve Common, so that the river and the houses are now on your left.

You are in a field that rises to the right, with a hedge to the left. Continue until you reach a row of trees and a broken down fence with a gate that you pass through. Ignore the yellow arrow pointing up the field to the right and walk forward towards another stile set is a fence slightly up the field. There will be a single house to your right and to the left, tall trees and the river. Cross the stile and head for a telegraph pole which bears a yellow band around it, and continue until another gate and stile are evident in the corner. Crossing this takes you down to a good gravel track. Take this, going left and straight, with a pond, evidently artificial judging by the device, an oxidiser perhaps, that floats on its surface. The gravel becomes concrete and takes you past some bungalows on the right. Soon the roadway forks - the left fork goes down to the river, but you want the right hand one that leads into the yard, which is part of the paper mill.

Don't feel apprehensive about walking the short distance through the property, as the right of way passes straight through the works and is partly waymarked, but please observe the NO SMOKING signs. This is the only surviving paper mill in the county. Continue straight through the yard, ignore another road that winds up to the right, and walk beneath a canopy that juts out from a loading bay on the left. Where this covered walkway ends, do not bear left, which would take you into one of the workshops, but bear right between some buildings. Doing so will take you into an open space with, on the right, a road that leads up and off the premises, a red brick office in front, and another office to the left with signs asking visitors to drive slowly because of the speed ramps, and to report to reception, neither of which apply to you. Instead, turn left, go between the two offices and bear right into a car park behind the brick building. Walk across the car park towards a gate with a yellow arrow on it.

The track beyond the gate soon bears to the left, and passes a gate on the left leading into a field and up to a farm, which you should ignore. Carry on, with a stream to the left, and head into a scrub, disregarding a track on the right. The way should be indicated by yellow markers on the trees. The path bears left to a slab that acts as a bridge over the stream. Cross this into a field. Turn immediately right and follow the perimeter of the field with the woods to the right. To the left the fields slope up to a farm. Where the wood appears to peter out, you will see another stile in a dog-leg' corner before you. Take this, heading for the old barn in front, with the stream to the right and a solitary house on the brow of the hill to the left. Cross one stile, walk behind the barn and cross another stile which leaves you on a path that is lined by a fence on one side and a hedge on the other, beyond which is a terrace of houses, the first sign of Postlip Hall. The path leads onto a metalled road, on the other side of which stands a gate. Go over or through this into a field that banks steeply up to the left and whose surface is crinkled with warrens. On the right is a high wall concealing Postlip Hall (for information on the hall, please see the first Cleeve Common walk).

Follow the wall as it curves round to the right and through a small wooden gate. Now you are on a firm track - there are stables and a converted mill to the left and an entrance affording a good view of the hall, to the right. Cross the track, pass through a succession of gates and follow the path round with the wall to the right, noticing the old well-spring in the field to the left, and the wooden gateposts leading towards the hall on the right.

The path ends with a gate at the base of Cleeve Common. Once through the gate, head upwards diagonally to the right towards the crest of the hill. At the top of the rise, you will meet another crossroads, where you go through a gate carrying a yellow waymark. head straight on and keep climbing until you meet a gate which will bring you on to the golf course. Continue forward past the clubhouse on the right and then the disused quarry. The farm and stables reappear, round which you turn right and descent to the road from which you started the walk.

The following two walks are rather dissimilar in character, although of roughly the same length. The first, apart from the initial climb, is the gentler; the second is marginally shorter but rather more strenuous.

'THE ROAD TO SUDELEY',
VINEYARD STREET, WINCHCOMBE, GLOS.

REARDON

LECKHAMPTON, SEVEN SPRINGS and COBERLEY
Distance 6 miles

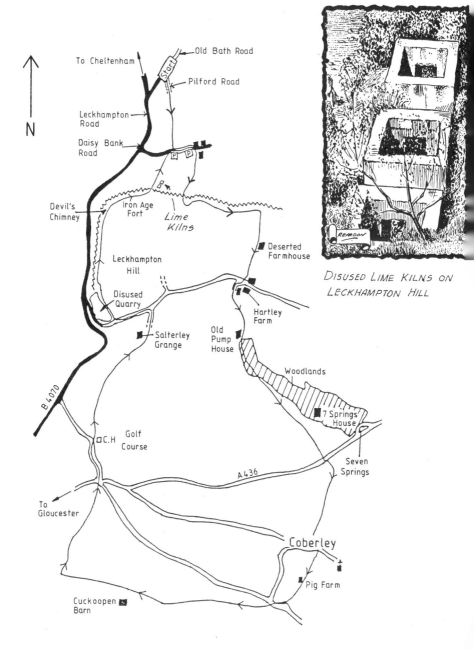

N

To Cheltenham

Old Bath Road

Start

Pilford Road

Leckhampton Road

Daisy Bank Road

P P

Devil's Chimney

Iron Age Fort

Lime Kilns

Deserted Farmhouse

Leckhampton Hill

Disused Quarry

Hartley Farm

Salterley Grange

Old Pump House

Woodlands

B.4070

C.H

Golf Course

7 Springs House

Seven Springs

A436

To Gloucester

Coberley

Pig Farm

Cuckoopen Barn

REARDON

DISUSED LIME KILNS ON LECKHAMPTON HILL

26

LECKHAMPTON, COBERLEY AND SEVEN SPRINGS

O.S. Landranger series on. 163

Starting point Grid Reference no: 949189

A circuitous walk of about 6 miles in which you will partake of some of the finest views in rural England; visit if you so wish the mythical source of the Thames; see the final resting place of Dick Whittington's mother; and commune with the devil himself. Allow three to three and a half hours.

Arriving by Bus: The Metro buses run a service (Route no.L) from the town centre to Leckhampton. Alight at the junction of Old Bath Road and Leckhampton Hill and walk back down Old Bath Road to a turning on the right, this is Pilford Road.

Walk up Pilford Road to the top, and cross a stile into a field and bear a little right towards some thorn bushes some 200 yards beyond. Continue up the centre of the field to a bank at the top. Turn right along this and cross a stile on the left in the corner. After a few yards, cross another stile to Daisy Bank Road, just opposite the second car park.

Arriving by Car: There are two cars parks along Daisy Bank Road. The first is bigger and off the road, the second is a large lay-by nearer to the point where the walk begins.

Walk beyond the second car park for about 100 yards, until some houses appear on the left. Between the first two is a path leading up from Cheltenham below. Opposite, to your right, the path continues upwards to Leckhampton Hill via a gap in the trees and some steps. Take this, which is quite steep, with woodland to your right and a high wooden fence appearing to the left. After 50 yards the path opens up among scattered trees that fall away to the right, with some thicket to the left and fields beyond it. Keep to the left. Where the trees come to an end, the path forks. The left fork appears to go straight on, but the right one, which seems to head up to the crest of the hill, is the one you want. Continue around a disused quarry to the left. Looking down towards Cheltenham, but slightly to the right will reveal a large white house, the recently refurbished Cheltenham Park Hotel. To its right are the flags and polished greens of Lilley Brook Golf Course. Nearby is Charlton Kings parish church, and in the far distance the radio masts of Cleeve Hill are clearly visible.

Around the corner from the quarry, the path forks yet again. Although the right hand fork appears to descend at first, this is the one that you want. Bear right until you arrive in a small clearing with a wooden bench.

Looking out across the vale at the same angle as the bench, you can see the Malvern Hills on a clear day in the far distance. To their left, but in the near distance, beyond the main Gloucester highway, is Staverton Airport, its runway and terminal seemingly stencilled onto the landscape. By looking to your extreme left, but just before the trees obstruct the view, you can see a hill on the skyline with what looks like a single giant mushroom sprouting from its summit. On closer inspection, this landmark is an outcrop of trees on property belonging to the National Trust and represents the highest point of the Forest of Dean. This is May Hill.

After a moment of contemplation, turn around and bear left up the hill. Once at the top, turn left towards the escarpment as it arcs away from you towards the golf course below. Now you are on Hartley Hill, part of the same geological outcrop that gives rise to Leckhampton Hill behind and Charlton Kings Common before you. Walk forward along the edge of the escarpment, with the stringy uncropped grasses and a row of trees to the right, until the main path seems to descend a little to the left. You, however, should keep right and follow a path through the bushes, until, not long after, a stile will appear on the shelf above you to the right, roughly where the trees finish. Going over the stile will take

27

you into a narrow defile between a wire fence and a stone wall. From the comparative wilderness behind, you have stepped into the calm, orderly world of arable farming.

Continue forward to where the stone wall gives out, although the foundations are still plainly visible, and go through a gate on the left, round a stile that has fallen into disrepair. Once through the gate, bear right towards the stone ruin, passing it by (noticing that the timbers of the hearth are still in place) and taking a stile on to a farm track. Follow this to the cluster of buildings ahead belonging to Hartley Farm. The barn ahead of you has a weather cock on its roof - turn right on to the road and walk past the first turning to the left, which leads to the farm house. Just after, is a sign pointing the way into a field on the left. Follow this, so that the line of trees and the farm is on the left, and pass two gates. The third opening on your left is a stile. Cross this into a field and go half right towards a plantation half way down the field . Bear right around the plantation (you are now in Hartley Bottom) and head towards an old pumping house. There will be a cottage and coppice above you to the left. Bestride the stile and continue forward with a mossy wall and wood to the left. Ignore the next stile, which will appear to the left and is watched over by a towering pylon. Carry on a little further until you find another stile on the left, which you should take, leaving you in a pretty meadow that sweeps gracefully in an arc between two woods. Take the stile and walk straight on, noticing the playing fields that will appear in front of you. Set back beyond the playing fields is Seven Springs House, built in the 1850's as the gift of a wealthy man to his daughter, and now an adventure school run by Gloucestershire County Council.

Carry on past the playing fields on your left until you come to a stile in the corner ahead of you. Take this and walk straight on with a high hedge to your left. There is a slight gradient here and when you reach the brow of the slope, all the fat of Gloucestershire's cultivated land opens up before you. By continuing straight, you will meet a stile in the corner of the field where it meets a metalled road, the A436 to Gloucester. Please take particular care when crossing this road and turn left. Within 10 yards you will see a sign with the barely discernible figures of a horse and rider pictured on it, pointing the way to Coberley. Turn right here and follow the path along the edge of the field until the corner, where you should turn right (and not go into the field ahead of you). The walk continues on to Coberley, but a diversion (of a half a mile, all told) may be made here for those who wish. For those who do not, skip the next paragraph.

THE SOURCE OF THE THAMES AND AN INN.

At this corner it is possible to turn left over a stile and head half left diagonally across the field to a metal kissing gate at the roadside about 100 yards from the spring, crossing another stile in the process. You may find that the path is marked out by means of a wire enclosure. In any case, once on the road (the A436) turn right and after 100 yards you will see a lay-by looping around a shallow hollow shaded by trees. This is 'Seven Springs', from where the River Churn rises, the longest tributary of the Thames. The official source of the Thames is deemed to be at Thames Head which lies to the south-west of Cirencester but the locals and other experts claim that it really springs from here. A plaque is built into the brickwork and inscribed thus : 'HIC TUUS O TAMESINE PATER SEPTEMGEMINUS FONS'. With the worn stone steps curving into the hollow, its mossy stone wall, and the trees leaning protectively over it, it is a pleasant scene, despite the proximity of the road. Opposite is the Seven Springs Inn, a free house with lunches of good reputation. It is an immense converted barn and sports a grand piano. To continue the walk, retrace your steps to the end of the last paragraph.

RESUMING THE WALK.

Turn right at the corner of the field and keep walking with a hedge to the left until you come to a junction of entrances to fields. Carry straight on into a sunken lane and head for the buildings ahead. As you enter Coberley village, notice the Church of England school on the right, an unusual convenience today in a village so tiny. Then you will come to the green and its stone cross; bear left here and then almost immediately after, you will see a narrow tarmac path on your right, insinuating itself between a group of trees on its left and a house on its right. This brings you down to another metalled road. Just to your left, is a post office, its scale in keeping with the size of the village. Sweets and refreshments are on sale here. The walk continues through the gate ahead of you, but another short diversion may be made in order to visit Coberley Church.

COBERLEY AND ITS CHURCH.

In order to reach St. Giles church, turn left and follow the road for about 400 yards until you see a group of buildings set back a little from the road to the right. The church, concealed from the road, is reached by going through a doorway and passing through a private garden. The name of the village comes from the old English 'Cuthberts glade'. The church lies outside the village proper. The oldest parts of the church are the West tower, the South porch and the South chapel, which date back to Norman times. In the sanctuary there is a heart-burial, the only one in the Cotswolds. The heart in question belonged to one Sir Giles Berkeley, a branch of the Berkeley family, who settled here and built a hall at the beginning of the 13th century. His son, Sir Thomas Berkeley, who fought at the Battle of Crecy, was married to Joan, and their effigies are to be found in the south chapel. Joan, on becoming a widow, was married again to Sir William Whittington. The fruit of their loins was Dick Whittington, who went on to become three times Lord Mayor of London. Coberely Hall used to stand next to the church and there are traces of its wall on its south side. The first was built in the early part of the 13th century by the Berkeley family, and Dick Whittington is said to have spent much of his childhood there. It was also where Charles 1 slept after the siege of Gloucester. A later version claimed that it was owned by a man who lost his fortune in the South Sea Bubble.

Now retrace your steps to the gate opposite the post office.

RESUMING THE WALK.

Go through the gate and down the path towards a stile. On the left is a spring which used to be the water supply for the village. At the bottom, cross the field. You will come to a pair of gates - take the right hand one into the farmyard. Keep to the track, with the wooden fence to the left and the buildings on the right. The track goes straight and then curves to the right, leading on to a metalled road. This farm is a 'trials and demonstration unit' specialising in pig breeding. The evidence is all around you!

Turning right along the road, continue for about 150 yards, and turn left off the road at a clump of trees to go through a gate on to a farm track that passes through the pig sties. Two tracks run parallel here - take the one on the left of the stone wall. Below you in the chasm lies Coldwell Bottom. Do not be tempted to branch off to the grassy track which skirts the valley, but keep to the track you are on as it rises up. Some way further on, you will come to a gate into an open field, with a clump of trees ahead of you. Here you should bear left along the grassier of the tracks that confront you, keeping alongside a fence and noticing the line of evenly spaced trees that have been planted as a windbreak on the ridge above you. As you go up to the brow of the hill, the Birdlip masts appear beyond a high stone wall. On your right, on the other side of the valley, you can see

Ullenwood Golf Course.

You will now come to a gate in the wall ahead. Go through this and walk straight across the field towards a wood in which the outline of Cuckoo Barn Farm can be espied. Continue past the entrance to the farm to the T-junction at the bottom of the field where you should turn right. The track takes you down with a stone wall and thicket to the left before emerging into open fields, with the clubhouse and the Ullenwood Star Centre for disabled ahead of you on the other side of the main road. Once you have arrived at the edge of the road, cross over and take the minor road ahead of you, that is signposted for the National Star Centre Ullenwood. This road takes you between Cotswold Hills Golf Course (it was moved here from its original site on Cleeve Hill) on the right and Ullenwood ('owls wood') Manor on the left. The manor was built in 1875 by the same man who built the Seven Springs House.

The road rises and bears left into the woods, before it curves away to the left over a bridge - but you want the bridlepath that leads away to the right from this corner, signposted 'Leckhampton Hill one and a quarter kms'. As the wide track strikes out from the road, you are following the golf course on the right. Ahead of you among the trees is Salterley Grange, and beyond are the contours of Leckhampton Hill. The track takes you through into the woods, passing the grange (the word Salterley means 'salt-dealers clearing') and the Ullenwood holiday chalets on the left. As the trees begin to dwindle, fields open out to the right, and you will soon come to a metalled road, the same indeed that was trod briefly at Hartley Farm. There are signs pointing back to Ullenwood 1km., Shurdington Hill 2 and a half kms., and another indicating Coberley and Seven Springs.

Turn left here, with pasture on the left and open field to the right. After some 150 yards, you reach a narrow path that leads up steeply from the road to the right, towards Leckhampton Hill. A disused quarry materialises below you to the left, and as you climb, there are good views of the Vale of Gloucester. You find yourself on a grassy slope with fields and wall to the right; looking back, you see the ridge with the trees planted as a windbreak, last seen near Cuckoo Barn Farm, standing at attention across the skyline. The path will narrow, taking you closer to the escarpment edge; and at a point where the path narrows still more, keep straight, and follow the sign to the Devil's Chimney (although bearing up and right here will take you to the remains of the Iron Age fort described in the walk entitled 'Leckhampton Hill and the Devil's Chimney').

As you go, the grass thins out and the cliffs on the right loom closer. To your left, another hill becomes visible in the distance - this is Robins Wood Hill, distinguishable by the scars of the artificial ski slope, that runs down it. Soon the path narrows further, running between a couple of small hummocks. Just before this point, on the left below the shelf, is the Devil's Chimney (see the walk entitled 'Leckhampton Hill and Devil's Chimney). Now the path descends rather steeply in stages, bringing you into a clearing dotted with boulders and the ruins of old lime kilns, relics of the days when the quarries were worked. At the end of this clearing, a fairly wide track is seen to descend through the trees and will bring you back to where you began the walk on Daisy Bank Road.

PUB.

The nearest pub is the 'Wheatsheaf', on the Old Bath Road, about 200 yards beyond Pilford Road.

WOODLAND AND PASTURE, FROM CHARLTON KINGS TO DOWDSWELL

O.S. Landranger Series no. 163

Starting point Grid Reference no. 960215.

This is a circular walk of some five and a half miles, for which 3 - 4 hours should be allowed. In some ways this is the most demanding of all the walks, for it take you continually up and down. From Charlton Kings you will ascend to upland pastures, then descend to an important water source, from where the path climbs to a woody peak, along a ridge, and down to Charlton Kings once again.

This is a walk with visual charms, but above all it will suit those with strong legs and who simply love walking.

Arriving by Bus: Service S75 and the Metro buses A/B run a good service to Charlton Kings. Alight at Six Ways and walk up Reyworth Road to the start of the walk.

Arriving by Car: The walk starts in residential Ryeworth Road, just off the A40 in Charlton Kings. There are a number of suitable parking points.

The Walk

Charlton Kings is proud of being independent of Cheltenham, though the origins of its name (Saxon for 'peasant's farmstead) indicates that it was of humble origins. The addition of 'Kings' shows that it was originally Crown property (as opposed to Charlton Abbots which belonged to Winchcombe Abbey).

Walk along Ryeworth Road, away from the main London Road towards the hills that rise up ahead of you. Shortly you will pass a pub on the right (the Ryeworth Inn, a Whitbread house), but do not fear as there is another pub half way through the walk, when some refreshment may be welcome.

The road curves away to the right. Follow it until you meet the junction with Glenfall Way - in the distance you can see a field that dips down to a valley with, beyond it, a hill covered in woodland. Turn left at the junction and the immediately right on to a firm track. The track dips down and where it curves to the left towards a farm, enter the field on the right over a stile. Turn right and follow the edge of the field. As you walk on, the view to the left opens up to the hills beyond, and the River Chelt (it is not clear what is the origin of 'Chelt' - perhaps 'Celt's water meadow') has appeared to your right. Follow the perimeter of the field as it bears left and the Chelt with it, noticing shortly the gate and bridge that spans the river giving access to some new houses. Continue to follow the field's edge as the path, which is only barely visible, bears left and up, away from the river. Behind you the Leckhampton Hill escarpment rears up and to its right the visually jarring Eagle Star Insurance Building, the tallest building in Gloucestershire.

Soon there will be a stile before you. Cross this and follow the faint path to the summit of the field, keeping close to the right boundary. Shortly the hedge sweeps around to the right - follow it through the gateway (quite possibly without a gate) into another field. Continue until you come to a stile/gate, flanked to the left by a barbed wire fence. Once on the other side of the gate, turn right into a field and then immediately left, keeping a hedge and a broad ditch to the left. The field meets a thicket hedge that runs down to the right, towards a farm and road. Go through the gap you see before you in the thicket, keeping to the top of the field, still with hedge and ditch to the left. Not long after you will see a gate and a stile ahead of you with th letter FP written upon it. Bestride this into a long narrow field of tufty pasture. Keep roughly to the right of the field, since you will eventually be going through a gate on this side, though not the farm gate that you will see fairly soon on your right.

WOODLAND and PASTURE
Distance 5½ miles

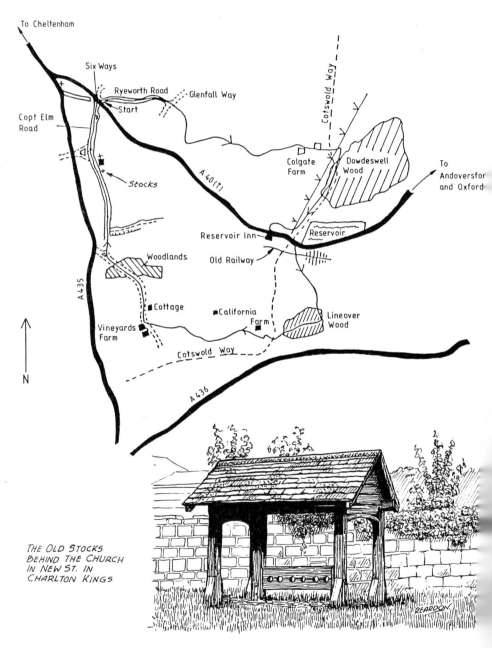

To Cheltenham

Six Ways

Ryeworth Road

Glenfall Way

Start

Copt Elm Road

Stocks

A 40 (T)

Colgate Farm

Dowdeswell Wood

Cotswold Way

To Andoversfor and Oxford

Reservoir Inn

Reservoir

Old Railway

Woodlands

A 435

Cottage

California Farm

Lineover Wood

Vineyards Farm

Cotswold Way

N

A 436

THE OLD STOCKS
BEHIND THE CHURCH
IN NEW ST. IN
CHARLTON KINGS

REARDON.

Some 70 yards or so before reaching the end of the field, look for and pass through a small wooden gate, set in the hedge to the right just before a grassy knoll. Ignore the similar gate that is visible ahead of you at the far end. Once through the gate, turn left and head towards the leftermost of two pylons, following the curve of a wooded hummock on your left. Very quickly Colgate Farm appears to the left. Enter the farmyard and follow the track to the right of the new barn and round towards a new bungalow. Continue past it, ignoring a track on the right. The track rises fairly steeply up past a cluster of barns on the left. At this point, underneath the pylon cables, there are stiles on the left and right, with arrows indicating that you are on the Cotswold Way. Take the one on the right that leads into a plantation - there is a string of conifers on your right and hedge to the left, looking down on to the village of Whittington. Follow the main path, which is clearly waymarked. After about 100 yards or so, ignore the path that shears off to the right down the hill and keep to the upper path which will take you past a plantation on your left This is Dowdeswell Wood, formerly filled with Oak, Ash and Elm, which was clear-felled during the 1970's to make way for conifers. There are signs telling you what trees are to be seen (some Beech, Scots Pine and Lawsons Cypress) but no amount of edification will ever replace the beauty of a wild wood. Amidst all this orderliness, the ghost of the last man to be hanged for sheep stealing is said to walk.

The path bears hard right and dips through a stile. Take it and turn immediately left, taking care not to slip on the steps on your way down. After about ten minutes Dowdeswell Reservoir will appear to your left and the A40 beyond it. The path fetches up underneath the reservoir bank, just past the cottage called Langate. Turn left over the sluice gate and then right, following the path around to the right, to where it meets the road. Dowdeswell is a compensation reservoir, built towards the end of the 19th century to satisfy the needs of a growing town when new wells would have proved inadequate. The A40 highway was developed as a mail coach route.

Turn left at the road, go past the Reservoir Inn (or stop in if you desire - it has been known to be open for breakfast and coffee from 9.30am and for drinks according to the old pub hours), and after about 250 yards cross the road to a track on the right, signposted for the Cotswold Way and 'Seven Springs and Leckhampton Hill'. After about 60 yards you will come to a gate and a stile, partly supported by the use of old rail tracks. Here, along this bank, the Banbury-Cheltenham railway line, inaugurated in 1889, used to run until its demise in 1963.

Cross the old line to another gate and stile and enter the field ahead of you keeping to the hedge on the left. Keep straight, heading for the hill in front of you. As you mount the field, any breathless moments can be used to take in the views around you! Soon there will be a stile with the words 'Woodland Trust' inscribed upon it. In fact there are gates leading onto two tracks, the one on the right seeming to be for vehicles. Take the stile on the left on to a stony path. On your right, beyond a reedy line of trees, is conifer plantation and on the left, beyond the hedge, open farmland. Shortly the path becomes steeper and untreated. At the top of the path there are steps leading up to another stile into a field through which you carry on up, keeping cables to the right and hedge to the left. At the top of this field, the path curls left to a gate and a stile. Go over this, turn right, and follow the fence. After some 60 yards, another stile on the right will lead you into Lineover woods, in which Oak, Ash and Hazel are widespread. When confronted immediately by a fork in the path, take the right lane which descends through airy woodland, the like of which has been in this spot for at least 600 years. Continue until a sort of clearing, currently being replanted. Bear right on a track through the trees, with the field fence on your right, and head down towards the farmhouse. After crossing a stile, head for a post that stands about 100 yards to the left of the barn. From the post (ignore the arrow that points to the left) you need to cut across the field more or less to the right until you reach an iron gate in the top right hand corner amongst some trees. Go through the gate and once into the field on the other side, turn left and follow the perimeter of the field which describes an immense arc below the upper escarpment, like the ridge of a bowl.

Below you is 'California' - the farm, that is!

By following the edge of the field almost to its end, you will pass through a gate on to an upward path, whereupon after about 50 yards, you arrive at a cross roads and another gate ahead of you with a B&B sign on it. Go through this and head directly across the field until you come to another B&B sign and a wide farm track leading down to the right. Follow the track down through a gate and past a farm. Pass the farmhouse on the left (this is Vineyard Farm, offering B&B), ignoring all entrances to it and head for a small metal gate inserted into the hedge ahead.

Turn right along the lane, towards the woods. Continue down the lane, passing some cottages on the right, until you come to a gate which takes you into a field. The path then curves around to the left, before it eventually takes you through a gate into the lush woods. Emerging from the woods, you will find yourself by a green surrounded by a triangle of narrow roads. Bear right and follow the road until it enters a residential area and crosses a bridge that spans an old railway cutting. Keep to this same road for quite some time eventually passing the entrance to a cemetery on the right, and then Charlton Kings church. Opposite the church is 'The Royal'. Pass the church until you see the memorial cross in front of it. Turn right here into Copt Elm Road and follow it all the way to the end, where is meets the A40. Opposite you, on the other side is Ryeworth Road, where you started the walk.

INDEX

Tourist Information Centre.
77 Promenade,
Cheltenham, GL50 1PP.
Tel: (0242) 522878

LOOK Out! for

our other products

Post Cards
Prints
Driveabout Packs
Post Card Packs
Cotswold Driveabout
Cotswold Driveabout - South
Calendars
and other drives and walks books

REARDON & SON

PUBLISHERS

56 Upper Norwood Street
Leckhampton
Cheltenham, Glos. GL53 0DU

Phone 23180
S.T.D. 024